WHY, GOD?

Calming Words for Chaotic Times

BY

CHARLES R. SWINDOLL

W PUBLISHING GROUP™

www.wpublishinggroup.com

A Division of Thomas Nelson, Inc.
www.ThomasNelson.com

WHY, GOD?

All scripture quotations in this book, except those noted
otherwise, are from the New American Standard Bible © 1960,
1962, 1963, 1971, 1973, 1975, and 1977 by the Lockman
Foundation, and are used by permission.

The *New International Version* of the Bible (NIV),
copyright © 1983 by the International Bible Society.
Used by permission of Zondervan Bible Publishers.

ISBN 0-8499-1757-3

Printed in the United States of America

05 04 03 02 01 PHX 5 4 3 2 1

Dedication

To all who died
as a result of
the atrocities committed
against us on
SEPTEMBER 11, 2001 . . .

and to all who live on
without their loved
ones by their sides.

Contents

Why, God?

OH LORD,

WHEN MY ANXIOUS THOUGHTS

MULTIPLY WITHIN ME,

YOUR CONSOLATIONS

DELIGHT MY SOUL.

—PSALMS 94:19

ONE
WHY, GOD?

Why, O LORD, do you stand far off?
Why do you hide yourself in times of trouble?
—PSALM 10:1, NIV

THE DATE, SEPTEMBER 11, 2001, is forever etched in our national memory. That morning stands as the never-to-be-forgotten hour when time stood still as we stared in horror and disbelief. With calculated and unconscionable malice, beastly terrorists stabbed our nation repeatedly in the heart—the World Trade Center in New York, at the Pentagon in Washington, and along a quiet countryside in southwest Pennsylvania. Thousands of unsuspecting civilians were brutally murdered. Our fellow Americans bled and died,

1

some immediately, many slowly and painfully, all unexpectedly. Others bravely escaped with their lives bruised, broken, and burned. In my mind, there isn't a hell hot enough for the cowards who perpetrated these vicious and brutal crimes against innocent victims. May the pain of their everlasting punishment know no bounds and find no relief.

And we cry out, "Why, God?"

I have studied the Revolutionary War and, in depth, the War Between the States. I have lived through World War II, the Korean War, the Lebanon Crisis, the Vietnam War, and the Persian Gulf War. I have watched drug-crazed hippies in their communes, angry students in campus riots, and lying leaders in the Watergate scandal, followed by a shocking presidential resignation.

I have blushed over immoral and unethical acts committed by religious leaders, traitors, politicians, and even presidents. I have witnessed racial hatred, been sickened by phony hypocrites, and waded through

depraved and unspeakable accounts of serial killers, mass murders, prison riots, domestic violence, and child molestations. These eyes have seen pictures of the holocaust victims from the Nazi regime and tragic torturings of prisoners of war.

"Why, God? Why?"

I have watched films of the landings at Iwo Jima, Tarawa, Guadalcanal, and the Normandy coastline on D-Day. I've shouted for joy over the fall of the Iron Curtain. I have also shuddered in dismay through chilling stories of the Khmer Rouge in the killing fields of Cambodia with its landmines and stacks of skulls left in its wake.

I have lived to see presidential assassinations, prejudicial assassinations, political assassinations, and suicides.

I've examined the pictures of horrible explosions on Hiroshima and Nagasaki, in the harbor at Texas City, at the Olympic Village in Atlanta, at the Federal Building in Oklahoma City, in the cafés and streets of Israel, and in the air as the Challenger disintegrated.

3

And with tears running down my face, I ask again, "O Lord, why?"

In my sixty-seven years on this earth I thought I had just about seen it all . . . until September 11, 2001. On that day I got a new understanding of the total depravity of humanity. And, as a byproduct, I have a new appreciation for the gifts of liberty and life itself—for the love of my wife, my family, and my friends—and for the power of the human spirit to press on and to recover from tragedy, no matter the sacrifice or cost.

Now we are, once again, at war as a nation. Our enemy is demonic and deceitful. Though identified by the frightening sounding name "terrorism," he is a coward to the core. He tries his best to intimidate us through repeated and savage acts of aggression and thereby paralyze us in fear. We witnessed on September 11 the limitless depths to which he will go to bring us down. But America will neither fear nor fail. We will not consider any sacrifice too great or any cost too high. Because we know that in the end God always wins, we

know we will win. As a brave brother of the faith wrote over five hundred years ago, "His rage we can endure, for lo his doom is sure."

And so, let us follow our earthly commander in chief with fidelity and loyalty. Let us walk directly into the sneer of the enemy with relentless resolve. Let us kneel before the Lord our Sovereign God with fresh faith. Let us trust Him through Jesus Christ our Savior with repentant hearts, with quiet confidence, and absolute dependence. By doing these things we can be certain of this final outcome, as the Psalmist once declared: "Through God we shall do valiantly" (Psalm 60:12).

Still, in our heart of hearts we whisper, "Why, God?"

Two
Brought to Our Knees

O God, our help in ages past,
Our hope for years to come
Be Thou our guide while life shall last,
And our eternal home!
—Isaac Watts

TIME, LIKE AN EVER-ROLLING STREAM, takes all its sons away. As never before in this generation, we realize that we are dependent upon God for protection and strength. Though the mountains quake, though bridges fall, though tunnels are destroyed, though ships sink, though lives will be lost, though war threatens to invade, though there may even be terrorists and enemies in our midst, we will *not* fear. Our resolve is firm because our refuge is based on the eternal foundation of the living God.

In the fourth volume of his immortal work, *Lincoln in the War Years*, author Carl Sandburg addressed the events that not only led up to our nation's sixteenth president's assassination but also, of course, the events that followed. It's a magnificent account written by Sandburg, a true wordsmith. All who love history know that the assassination of Lincoln took place on the fourteenth of April, 1865. You may not remember that it was Good Friday. The president was officially pronounced dead the following day, the fifteenth of April, the day before Easter.

When Sandburg picked up his pen to write the seventy-fifth chapter, he was searching for a title that would say it best as he attempted to summarize the life of Lincoln in an appropriate way. In doing so, he went to an old, plain proverb that was often used among woodsmen as he titled the chapter "A Tree Is Best Measured When It's Down." As Sandburg measured the tree, he wrote not only of the now-dead president, he also wrote of preachers on that Easter Sunday following the death of Lincoln. He wrote,

On the Saturday following Good Friday, thousands of sermons were laid away as of no use for Easter Sunday. A new sermon had to be written or extemporized after the news arrived on Saturday forenoon or afternoon that the President was dead. The pastor who failed to deal with the national grief heard from his flock.

In great stone cathedrals of the cities, in modest framed churches of small towns, in little cabin churches at country crossroads, in hospital chapels and in at least one state prison, on Navy ships and in outdoor army-camp services, there were Easter Sunday sermons memorializing the dead President.[1]

There was an outpouring from thousands of pulpits; pulpits from coast to coast rather uniformly dealt with varied aspects of their grief.

I thought as I recently reread that account, *It is amazing how history repeats itself*. It was not on a Saturday that the tragic events transpired which

brought us to our knees. And the Sunday that followed was not Easter Sunday, but I can assure you that preachers all over the world scrambled to change their sermons for Sunday, September 16, 2001. The series that I was presenting at the time on the life of the apostle Paul seemed strangely irrelevant in light of our times. Like all other pastors around the globe, I changed directions and immediately began to pursue the events in which we found ourselves in hopes of finding some calming words for our chaotic times. I found them in the Book of Psalms.

---

[1] Carl Sandburg, *Lincoln in the War Years*. Harcourt, Brace and Company, 1939.

THREE
A CHRONICLE OF CHAOS

I have become like broken pottery. . . .
there is terror on every side.
—PSALM 31:12–13, NIV

I T WAS NOT JUST ONE ACT of treacherous terrorism that stunned us on September the eleventh; it was several. To make matters worse, these several attacks were carried out in a carefully planned sequential strategy of brutal destruction. And before the smoke cleared, we were stunned to discover that there were other planned assaults on our national leaders that, gratefully, failed to materialize that same day. I shudder, literally shudder, when I pause to think of how much more terrible it could have been if the demonic plot had run its course as had been devised in the original scheme of evil, demented minds.

If I repeat just a two-hour-and-thirty-one-minute log of the events of that morning in rapid-fire fashion, you will have sufficient information to remember what transpired that frightening morning. The times I refer to are based on central standard time.

At 6:58 A.M., United Airlines Flight 175 left Boston bound for Los Angeles with 56 passengers, 2 pilots, and 7 flight attendants.

One minute later, at 6:59 A.M., American Airlines Flight 11 departed from Boston en route to Los Angeles with 81 passengers, 2 pilots, and 9 flight attendants.

Two minutes later, at 7:01 A.M., United Airlines Flight 93 left Newark, New Jersey, headed for San Francisco with 38 passengers, 2 pilots, and 5 flight attendants.

Nine minutes later, at 7:10 A.M., American Airlines

Flight 77 took off from Dulles International Airport bound for Los Angeles with 58 passengers, 2 pilots, and 4 flight attendants.

Thirty-five minutes later, at 7:45 A.M., American Flight 11 plunged into the north tower of the World Trade Center in Manhattan—a direct hit.

Eighteen minutes after the north tower was hit, at 8:03 A.M., United Flight 175 crashed into the south tower of the World Trade Center.

Forty minutes after the south tower was hit, at 8:43 A.M., American Flight 77 crashed into the Pentagon. A hole at least two hundred feet wide was ripped open on the west side, and flames burst forth from the nerve center of our nation's major military building.

Seven minutes after the Pentagon was hit, at 8:50 A.M., the south tower of the World Trade Center collapsed.

Eight minutes later, at 8:58 A.M., an emergency dispatcher in Westmoreland County, Pennsylvania, received a cell phone call from a man who said he was

a passenger locked in the bathroom of United Flight 93. The dispatcher quoted the man as saying, "We are being hijacked! We are being hijacked!" The man then said the plane was going down and reported some sort of explosion and white smoke coming from the plane. At that moment the dispatchers lost contact with him.

Twelve minutes after that cell phone call, at 9:10 A.M., United Flight 93 from Newark to San Francisco crashed near Summerset, Pennsylvania, eighty miles southeast of Pittsburgh. Representative James Moran of Virginia, after a Marine Corps briefing, said that hijackers evidently planned to crash the plane into the presidential retreat at Camp David or the United States Capitol.

At that same moment, 9:10 A.M., a portion of the Pentagon collapsed.

Only 19 minutes after the Pentagon's west side collapsed, at 9:29 A.M., the north tower of the World Trade Center collapsed.

I thought I had already lived through America's worst disasters. How wrong I was. Many other significant

events could be named, but that gives you sufficient evidence of how these atrocities happened back-to-back-to-back-to-back. Right on schedule, planned to the point of precision, the horrible events ran their course. "Why, God?" was the question most people were asking.

At 7:30 that same evening, as millions of Americans met in places of worship to pray, our president briefly addressed the nation, which we all saw, and tape recorded for later viewing. One statement he made stood out in my mind then and still lingers today: "Terrorist attacks can shake the foundations of our biggest buildings, but they cannot touch the foundations of America."

FOUR
HOW FIRM A FOUNDATION

"If the foundations are destroyed,
What can the righteous do?"
—PSALM 11:3

A S I SAT AND LISTENED to President Bush that
somber night, I remembered a Psalm I had
studied years ago. You know how things stay in
your mind, and you snag them with another thought
years later, then go back and regather that first event?
That's what happened. While doing a study on
"Selected Psalms" many years ago, I remember a question that was asked that used a word from the president's speech, and it stuck in my mind.

The question is asked in Psalm 11. Go with me for

just a glance. David wrote Psalm 11, probably while he was being hunted and haunted by King Saul. With borderline insane paranoia, Saul began seeking the life of David, believing the young man was out to get him and take his position as king. David is on the run. As he writes in the first part of this psalm, he has flown as a bird to the mountain. And in that hiding place, momentarily removed from danger, he asks this question: "If the foundations are destroyed, what can the righteous do" (v. 3)?

Great question! Webster tells us that a "foundation" is "the basis upon which something stands or is supported." Every house has a foundation. Every significant structure, every building has a foundation. The taller the building, the deeper and more important the foundation. Destroy the building's foundation, and you've toppled the building.

Funny, isn't it, how words repeat themselves on other lips? I was watching the national prayer service in which Dr. Billy Graham, our nation's esteemed

evangelist and spokesman for Christ, referred to the structures the terrorists destroyed. He stated that the twin towers may have been destroyed, but their foundations, amazingly, were still in place. He then spoke with great relief for our nation, saying, "It's the same with us. If our foundations are in place, then nothing else really matters."

That is precisely David's point. David is not referring to structures. No house or building is in his mind, and there is no reference to such in this psalm. This psalm is about life. The righteous stand on a firm foundation. Now, should the foundation of a life be destroyed, that life crumbles. But if the foundation remains secure, no amount of stress—in David's case, no ugly attack on his life by Saul or any of his troops—would cause his life to fracture or crumble. You see, David is viewing the treacherous, threatening words of Saul as arrows coming from warriors. He uses a vivid word picture in the second verse: "Behold, the wicked bend the bow, they make ready their arrow upon the string. . . ."

17

In those days the warrior was known for his keen ability with bow and arrow. One of the most effective weapons in David's day was a sharp, slender arrow as it slipped from the bow guided by the marksman's eye to the target. David's point is that the wicked are bending bows, and they are making ready their deadly arrows on the string. I don't think David had a literal bow and arrow in mind. He was thinking in terms of words shot at him or statements made against him, as part of the plot planned to bring him down. But that won't happen to him if the foundations of his life are strong and secure.

However, if those foundations are destroyed, his life collapses, drops like a sack of salt. How can I say that his foundations were solid and secure? Look at the first verse. Look at his opening statement. Occasionally, in the biblical psalms, as in newspaper columns, the gist of the whole message is in the first sentence, and everything that follows is an amplification of the initial sentence. This psalm is like that. David's main message is

in the first verse of this psalm: "In the LORD I take refuge; how can you say to my soul, 'Flee as a bird to your mountain.'"

My soul is not on the run. My spirit has not capsized, because in the Lord I take refuge. A refuge is a place of hiding. It is a place of protection. The term is *chasah*, in the ancient Hebrew. A *chasah* is a protective place that provides safety from that which would otherwise hit and hurt. It's a protection from danger and from distress. David makes it clear that *Yahweh* is his *chasah*. Since that is true, David says, "My foundations are sure."

The old country preacher was right when he said, "I may tremble on the rock, but the rock doesn't tremble under me." It is my solid foundation. It stands firm no matter what may occur.

That word "refuge" reminded me of yet another psalm—the forty-sixth. Who wouldn't find comfort in the solidarity of this ancient promise? This is the very psalm in which Martin Luther found refuge and relief

19

over five hundred years ago. He hid in its truths and found strength. Psalm 46 gave him fresh courage to go on, even though misunderstood, maligned, and mistreated. How comforting were those words, "God is our refuge" (*chasah*, same word) . . . "God is our refuge and strength, a very present help in trouble" (v. 1).

It was from the opening lines of this forty-sixth psalm that Luther later was inspired to write, *"Ein' Feste Burg Ist Unser Gott"*—"A high tower is the Lord our God." We sing those words today: "A mighty fortress is our God, a bulwark never failing." And why is such a foundation sure? Because it is God, Himself! Our foundation is the God of creation. The God who made us is the God who shelters us.

He who dwells in the secret place of the Most High shall abide under the shadow of the Almighty. [El Shaddai]

I will say of the LORD, "He is my refuge" [my *chasah*]
"and my fortress; My God, in Him I will trust."
—PSALM 91:1–2, NKJV

On that solid foundation, we are secure, no matter
how insecure and chaotic our times may be!

Five
A Very Present Help

God is our refuge and strength,

an ever-present help in trouble.

—Psalm 46:1

GOD IS OUR REFUGE AND STRENGTH. As Eugene Peterson paraphrases it in *The Message*, "God is a safe place to hide." *Chasah* is a word that's needed when a nation finds itself shaking on the rock. The news of terrorist attacks is enough to grab you by the neck and make you tremble. After the attack on America, I found myself not sleeping very well, not until I remembered Psalm 46 and called to mind my *chasah*, "a very present help in trouble."

Charles Spurgeon writes, "As God is all-sufficient,

our defense and our might are equal to all emergencies.
. . . He is not as the swallows that leave us in the winter; He is a Friend in need, and a Friend indeed. When it is very dark with us, let brave spirits say, 'Come, let us sing the forty-sixth!'"

> A fortress firm and steadfast rock,
> Is God in time of danger;
> A shield and sword in every shock,
> From foe well-known or stranger.[1]

Let's look deeper into this psalm. Like the eleventh, it makes its summary statement at the beginning, then everything else hangs on that. Think of the first verse as the coat hanger, and all the clothing (verses 2–11) hangs on that hanger. The hanger, remember, is that God is our refuge and a very present help when war is declared. God is a refuge and very present help when terrorists strike. God is a refuge and very present help when the bridge falls, or the tunnel caves in, or the dam

23

gives way, or the plane crashes. God is our refuge and strength, a very present help.

If you have a Bible handy, locate Psalm 46. Take a closer look at the structure of the psalm. You'll find the same word used three times. Let your eyes scan down through the words of the psalm and check the right margin. The end of verse three, *Selah*. The end of verse seven, *Selah*. And the end of the last verse, *Selah*. And so we find *Selah. Selah. Selah.*

The psalms were originally musical compositions. They provided the lyrics for inspired hymns. For years the church sang only from the Psalter. They literally sang the psalms—the songs of David, Moses, Korah, and others provided the first hymnal for God's people.

I have an old, old songbook, if you can call it that. It is comprised of just words of psalms that were sung in an old church so many, many years ago. In old English, it is simply called *The Psalter*.

God's people gathered and sang from *The Psalter*. This notation is written at the beginning of Psalm 46:

"for the choir director. A Psalm of the sons of Korah, set to Alamoth. A Song." "*Alma*" is the original Hebrew term, translated "maiden" or "young woman." It probably means it was composed to be sung as a high-pitched song. It was reserved for the sopranos or for the stringed instruments that played in the upper part of the treble clef. It's not unlike Handel's opening recitative "Comfort ye, comfort ye My people" sung by a lyric tenor soloist, and that leads into, "Every valley shall be exalted and every mountain and hill made low, the crooked places straight and the rough places plain." It's a beautiful composition written for the high voices. So if you sing soprano, this psalm is for you especially.

But never forget, it is a psalm of God's *chasah*. He is our refuge, and what comfort that brings! He is your refuge even when you are all alone. He is your refuge when you awaken in the night filled with fear, and cold sweat breaks out. He is your refuge, your strength, a very present help when events transpire that you cannot understand. When your boy is on that aircraft carrier steaming toward the war zone, when your son or daughter is climbing aboard that fighter plane, pulling the cockpit closed and giving the "thumbs up" before takeoff, He is your very present help. When? "In trouble." When you read the next headline, and it tells of some event that you and I would call tragic, He is a very present help. *Selah!*

Meaning what? Well, as best we can tell, *Selah* was an ancient musical notation. Music scores today have unique notations or signs that musicians understand. Some look like arrowheads pointing left or right signifying to the musician to increase or diminish the volume. In biblical days *selah* probably meant "pause." I have a friend who, every time he reads the Psalms and comes across *selah*, he simply reads, "Pause and let that sink in." Not bad.

These three *selahs* give us the structure of the psalm. Verses two and three refer to times of *physical catastrophe*. *Selah.* Pause, and here's how to handle such things. Verses four through seven refer to the *threat of warfare*.

Selah. "Pause, let that sink in. This is how to respond to that." And in verses eight through eleven, when the future seems uncertain, this is how you handle that. *Selah*. "Pause and let that sink in."

Don't panic; pause.

No need to fret and fear; pause.

And in place of worry and anxiety, pause. The foundation is firm. The Lord is our refuge. He is our present help in trouble.

Pause, let that sink in.

---

[1] Spurgeon, Charles. From a sermon, 1887.

Six
No Fear!

We will not fear, though the earth give way
and the mountains fall into the heart of the sea.
—Psalm 46:2, NIV

IN TIMES OF PHYSICAL CATASTROPHE like the
recent atrocities, what is our response? Usually, it's
"Why, God? Why me? Why us?" In contrast, God's
Word says in times of physical catastrophe, "we will not
fear" (Psalm 46:2). Take the time to observe that the
examples are all introduced with "though." "Though
the earth should change, though the mountains slip
into the heart of the sea." Referring to what?

Though there may be an earthquake, and the
ground moves beneath you. "Though its waters roar and

foam . . ." That would have reference to a flood, a tsunami, a tidal wave, the waters from a swelling river after the snow melts, or the rain that doesn't stop falling. He goes further—another catastrophe. Though the mountains quake at its swelling pride." An avalanche! That horrible moment of looking up and seeing the tons of snow and debris, ice and rock plunging toward you. Our response? Since God is our refuge, we will not fear.

Why not? Let me repeat the promise, which makes our foundation firm. It's because the Lord our God is our *chasah*. He is our refuge, He is our strength. He's the rock. It surprises all of us, but it's no surprise to Him. Hear that, open theists. Hear that, all you who say that God is surprised by such events, having just discovered what has happened on this earth. *(Give me a break!)* Our God is in sovereign control of all the events of this earth. They occur exactly as He has planned or permitted them.

Then how can I explain why bad things happen? How can I resolve the ringing question, "Why, God?" I did not say our Father has explained Himself. (How,

in fact, can an infinite God ever explain Himself to finite people?) I said our Father has planned or permitted the events of this earth. He has no obligation to explain Himself. The Creator does not explain why to the created. It would be like a brilliant potter explaining himself to a mass of soft clay.

Nothing surprises God. What puzzles us is permitted by our Lord, for reasons too profound to grasp. It is put together in the counsel of His own will so that it fits perfectly into His plan for His glory and for His purposes. As His servant, I say in response, "I will not fear. Though I don't understand it, I will not fear. Though You take something that's deeply significant to me, though You allow a catastrophe to strike, I will not fear. I will not blame, I will not doubt, and I will not question." There will be no out-of-control anxieties. Why? Because God is our refuge. There will be no exaggerated feelings of uneasiness, because God is our refuge. There will be no middle-of-the-night shakes. Why? Because God is our refuge. There will be no morning dread or

evening desperation or lingering depression. Why? Because *God is our refuge*.

Martin Luther connected those dots:

> And though this world with devils filled,
> Should threaten to undo us,
> We will not fear, for God hath willed
> His truth to triumph through us.[1]

The answer is not complicated. *Selah*. Pause. Rest easy. Don't expect life to make sense. Don't fear because surprises occur. Life is full of surprises, shocks, and insanities.

While feeling disturbed last night over the current atrocities that were perpetrated against our country and entertaining a growing anxiety over the probability of further terrorist attacks on more innocent defenseless people, I tossed and turned in bed, unable to sleep. I got up, walked into my study, slumped into my leather chair, and stared at my shelves of books. The small lamp we leave lit through the night gave me enough light to read one title after another.

Suddenly, my eyes shifted to my computer screen. I noticed an unopened e-mail message from a long-time friend who lives in Southern California. I clicked into it and was relieved. Among other things he asked a simple question: "Have you noticed the insights in Psalm 94:19?" Curious, I opened my Bible and read the verse: "When my anxious thoughts multiply within me, your consolations delight my soul."

Talk about a *selah* moment! A surge of refreshing peace rushed through me. I was reminded once again of Him who, alone, is my refuge and strength. I returned to bed and slept soundly until dawn.

But there is more, much more in Psalm 46. What about warfare? All Jews looked upon Jerusalem, especially in those days, as "the city of God (v. 4)." And so David, as he's hiding in the rocks not far from that great city where he had spent so many years of his life, pauses and reflects. He remembers the river that flows into the channels that irrigate the soil. He pictures in his mind's eye the crops and plants that grow there in that desert-like region, thanks to the flowing water. He calls the city the "holy dwelling places of the Most High" (v. 4). And again God emerges as paramount . . . *God* is the star of the event. "God is in the midst of her," he exclaims.

"God," verse five continues, "will help her when morning dawns" (when the attack comes from the enemy). See how he puts it? When "the nations made an uproar, the kingdoms tottered" (v. 6). It's the picture of the Assyrians, the Egyptians, and the other enemies as they would come in and tromp over Israel with heavy boots, assaulting and attempting to blast her into nonexistence. But it never happened. Why? Because of her refuge. God is in the midst of her. And the result is this: "She will not be moved" (v. 5).

We are not moved either. We are not moved, even though terrorists have come at us with their atrocious attacks and have hit the defenseless at a time when

they couldn't protect themselves. These murderers
came upon frightened men, women, and children in an
unsuspecting moment and, like a bully on the playground, beat them mercilessly. But even though the
assault was damaging, we have no reason to fear or to be
moved. Verse seven says, "The LORD of hosts is with us;
the God of Jacob is our stronghold. Selah."

When terrorists strike, your tendency is to read the
news more than you read your Bible. I would venture to
say you spent much more time watching the newscasts
following September 11 than you have spent reading
God's Word, right? We know the faces of the newscast-
ers on CNN better than we know the inspired and
encouraging words of David in the Psalms. And because
that is true we forget, "The LORD of hosts is with us; the
God of Jacob is our stronghold" (v. 7).

- How can I be sure?
- How can I not be moved?
- How can I not fear?
- How can I face an uncertain future?

Verse eight announces, "Come." It says, in effect, "Come here, psst, come here . . . come here." It's an invitation asking us to go back into history. Return to another time, a former era. Blow the dust off your memory.

Behold the works of the LORD,
Who has wrought desolations in the earth.
[Remember the past].

He makes wars to cease to the end of the earth;
He breaks the bow and cuts the spear in two;
He burns the chariots with fire. (vv. 8–9)

Those accounts of God's former deliverance are all written in the chronicles of history. You can read them for yourself. Consider our nation's history, beginning with the Revolutionary War. You'll get renewed courage all over again. You'll hear George Washington quoting verses of Scripture like a preacher in a pulpit. You will read incredible statements of faith from other political leaders from that era right on into the Civil War. The speeches of our national leaders were shaped with words about the Living God. How do you think Lincoln kept his senses in a time like that? He had the most unenviable presidential experience in the history of our nation. But he was not moved. And he did not fear, thanks to his numerous *selah* moments. *Selah.*

God says, "I will be exalted among the nations, I will be exalted in the earth" (v. 10). As David ends this section, he makes the same statement as when he concluded the psalm: "The LORD of hosts is with us; the God of Jacob is our stronghold. Selah."

We will not fear, though catastrophes occur. We will not be moved, though we are at war. Why? Because God—the omnipotent, all-powerful, magnificent God—is our refuge and strength.

---

[1] Luther, Martin. 1485–1546.

SEVEN
FACING AN UNCERTAIN FUTURE

Cease striving, and know that I am God.
—PSALM 46:10

HOW CAN WE FACE THE FOG of our uneasy, uncertain future? All these terrifying events are happening—buildings collapsing, explosions all around us, anthrax and bioterrorism threats which intensify our concerns. What more can the future hold?

Verse ten of Psalm 46 answers that. *We will not worry.* The text says, "cease striving . . ." The Hebrew simply uses one term in that command, and it means, "Stop!" What a great directive! STOP!

I heard a mother say that to one of her children in

the grocery store just yesterday. The child was busy, busy, busy. Getting into this, messing with that. "Stop!" When I heard her, *I stopped!*

But it's the Lord who is speaking at this moment. "Stop! Stop it! Stop that worrying. Quit it! I am your refuge. I am your very present help in time of trouble. Your worry implies that I'm not here anymore. But I never left. I'm not like the swallows that leave in the winter, to return only when the weather is fair."

Now you see why Psalm 46 speaks with such relevance. In times of physical catastrophe, since God is our refuge, we will not *fear*. At the threat of warfare, since God is our refuge, we will not *be moved*. With a future that seems uncertain, we will not *worry*. We'll remember He brings an end to wars. War is nothing new to Him. Chariots, spears, arrows have a way of making us churn within. But, *stop!* We will not worry.

I was reminded this past week that back in the days of the Revolutionary War it wasn't uncommon for pastors to preach sermons that prepared congregations for

battle, I mean literal battle. There was a war going on, and sermons were delivered to bring courage. Those sermons came to be known as "artillery sermons." Isn't that a good name? When a pastor preached with passion, you could almost hear the report of the artillery: *Kavoomm! Kavoomm!* Pastor's launching another artillery sermon today—*Kavoomm!* I love that!

Artillery sermons were preached by stouthearted, unintimidated pastors, who also served as leaders of the local militia. Artillery was viewed back then as the first-strike weapon, out in front of the infantry attack. They were designed to weaken the enemy's defense for the assault. In a similar way, artillery sermons were delivered to stir hearts, preparing people for battle. God's Word became the ammunition to weaken the enemy's position and to strengthen the Christian for literal as well as spiritual warfare in the days yet future.

If it would help you to think of this book in that way, consider this to be one of those *Kavoomm* messages. This is an artillery message, because some of you who read

these words have been afraid. No doubt, you have been moved over the recent events. You may be depressed and worried about the future, because you haven't been equipped with proper ammunition. But, in fact, no terrorist is able to destroy or defend against the truth of God.

If the foundations are in place, if we have the Lord God as our refuge and strength, the righteous do not fear, are not moved, and cannot worry.

Kavoom!

Eight
Identify the Enemy

Your enemy the devil prowls around like
a roaring lion looking for someone to devour.
— I Peter 5:8, NIV

N OW THAT THE ARTILLERY SERMON has revved us up, we want to charge into battle. But before you can march out against the enemy, you have to know who he is. It's called "gathering intelligence." You need to know how he operates, where his base of operations is, what his tactics are. You have to be able to identify him in all circumstances. Since September 11, we have seen and heard hundreds of reports on America's enemy. We have seen his face. We have heard his threats and innuendos. We have researched his hiding places and training camps. We know his name. We know his *modus operandi*. He is brilliant. Rich. Dangerous. And focused on destroying us, all in the name of his god. To him, it is *jihad*—holy war.

And while he is certainly our earthly enemy, he is not the enemy about whom we must be most concerned. No. "Your adversary," Peter clearly states, "is the devil." He is at the root of all evil. He is relentlessly engaged in a strategy to bring us down. With deceptive stealth, "he's like a roaring lion, seeking someone to devour" (1 Peter 5:8). Last time I checked, hunters called the lion the "king of beasts." The last time I did an investigation of the devil, he was the highest of all the angelic creatures. Though he fell from that exalted position due to pride, he didn't lose any of his brilliance. Make no mistake about it, when the highest of God's angelic creations fell, he instantly rolled up his sleeves and entered into conflict with the divine plan. Small wonder that we're told, "Be of sober spirit" (v. 8a). There's a war on! Once we identify

the enemy and understand his wicked ways, we realize the world is a battleground, not a playground.

Let me pause here and set the record straight. *First,* we're living in a culture that is politically correct but is theologically, ethically, and morally corrupt. To the very center of its being, today's culture is corrupt. Humanity without Christ is totally depraved. The world will lead you directly *away from* the things of God, rather than *toward* them.

Second, we are now facing hardships, conflicts, and trials like none of us would have ever imagined, because we are encountering our adversary on his turf. Everything God's people love, he hates. For instance, he hates your Christian marriage. Chances are good that more marriages are in conflict in these stressful days than in days past. Chances are you've got troubles in your family—more than usual. Perhaps one of your children is in open rebellion. If they're not there yet, it's just because they're not old enough. It's only a matter of time. Why? Our adversary hates harmony in the family.

Chances are the conflicts occurring in your occupation have reached such an intense level, you're ready to say, "I don't even know if Christianity works anymore." It's all part of the enemy's strategy.

Chances are you're going through a struggle emotionally or physically—either yourself, your mate, someone in your family, or one of your close friends.

Chances are very good that a grandchild or a great-grandchild is very sick right now. The devil hates strong minds, secure wills, and stable bodies.

We shall encounter enemy attacks in any number of areas. While we ought not to live in fear of it, we're not to be ignorant of it either. The enemy loves for you to be kept ignorant about him, to think of him inaccurately or with a shrug. He hates messages like this book. He is being identified for who he really is; he doesn't go for that.

Do you need some good news? It's found in this same section of Scripture. We can resist the enemy! Look closely yourself at the opening line of 1 Peter 5:9. "But

resist him, firm in your faith. . . ." The enemy's attacks may be directed toward the vulnerable part of your life, but the shield of faith will protect you from them. You *can* resist him!

Furthermore, realizing that God is our refuge, we can go to Him immediately. There's nothing like prayer to dislodge the darts of the enemy. And you're not alone. Verse nine states "your brethren" are experiencing the same sufferings you are. You're not unique. You are part of the groundswell of God's triumphant movement. But this counterstrategy carries with it severe tests. They're coming. Some have obviously already arrived (one hit hard on September 11—black Tuesday), and we are to be aware of others to come. My task is to equip you for them and to warn you ahead of time that more are coming—whatever they may be. If I knew, I would make a public announcement. But nobody knows. All we do know is that more will come our way. Our adversary never runs out of creative, deceptive ideas. But we will not fear, we will not be moved, we will not worry.

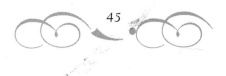

Peter offers even better news: "After you have suffered for a little while, the God of all grace, who called you to His eternal glory in Christ, will Himself . . ." [I love these four promises; look at the words.] ". . . perfect, confirm, strengthen and establish you" (1 Peter 5:10).

Don't miss the meaning of each term. He will "perfect" us in the suffering. This means He will restore us, bringing us to a new level of maturity.

Next, He will "confirm" us in the suffering. At the heart of this term is the concept of being made solid in our character. He will use the hardship to solidify our character.

And then we're told, He will "strengthen" us. The fatty flab brought on by easy living will be replaced with strong muscles of determination.

Finally, He will "establish" us. The Greek term suggests the idea of laying the foundations. The suffering will drive us deep to the bedrock of our faith.

And in the end, who is going to win? Read verse

eleven: "To Him be dominion forever and ever. Amen." We could add *Selah!*

"I believe it," says the apostle Peter. "I stake my trust in it. I stand on it. I can assure you when the hard times have run their course, your lives will be perfected, confirmed, strengthened, and stabilized." The adversary will continue his assaults and take his cheap shots. I need to tell you ahead of time, that's coming. But in the end, God wins.

In the amazing Book of Revelation, John vividly describes the enemy, his attacks, and the ultimate outcome. The war has already been won by the good guys. When Jesus died on the cross and rose again, it was all over for Satan. He was and is ultimately defeated. Still, he fights on. And yes, he wins a few battles along the way. But it doesn't matter, because he's lost the war.

It reminds me of wars past, when communications were poor. Sometimes, armies went on fighting for months after the war had officially ended, because they

didn't know they had already lost. So it is with Satan and his armies.

John basically stands toe to toe with the enemy, spits in his eye, and says, "Take your best shot, Satan. Do your worst. And we'll answer, 'Hallelujah anyway!' Because we know the victory is already ours."

Still, when Satan and his lieutenants attack us, we must do battle. We must gather up our courage from the Word of God and march out to meet the enemy face to face. But we go knowing we are already victorious.

Nine
Marching Orders

Humble yourselves, therefore, under God's mighty hand,
that he may lift you up in due time.

—I Peter 5:6, NIV

I WASN'T THERE when a few men gathered around him. General Dwight Eisenhower had the awful job on that day in early June 1944 of determining if that was the right day to make the most significant invasion in the history of military strategy.

The weather wasn't right.

The tide wasn't right.

The sea wasn't good.

The counsel wasn't unanimous.

In fact, some of his most trusted advisors urged, "No." But he said, "Let's go."

As we all know from history, those first few waves of soldiers were picked off by the enemy like sitting ducks. The wet sand on the beach was dyed crimson with the blood of great Americans as they landed and invaded the northern perimeter of France to take that area before moving on toward Berlin.

I have the distinct feeling that nobody sat around in a small group just before that first, second, or third wave hit the beach telling jokes. No one in an amphibious landing craft said, "Man, this will be fun! We're gonna have the time of our lives." No. Not that morning. There were real bullets in those rifles. There were real shells in those massive cannons. There were powerful landmines hidden along those shores. Bodies would be blown apart. Friends would die. It was serious stuff—as serious as a coronary—as they waded ashore, as some stumbled to shore over their own vomit, as others were blinded by explosives, scared half out of their wits. They knew this was for keeps. No more jokes, no more fun and games. The training was done. This was the real thing.

Isaac Watts's words may be old, but they have a twenty-first century ring of relevance. Ponder the questions he asks:

> Are there no foes for me to face?
> Must I not stem the flood?
> Is this vile world a friend to grace,
> To help me on to God?

Do you see the questions? Do I have foes? Can I escape? Is the world a friendly place? He answers firmly:

> Sure I must fight if I would reign:
> Increase my courage, Lord;
> I'll bear the toil, endure the pain,
> Supported by Thy word.

We face a very real, insidious enemy. To make things even more confusing, the source of all the evil is invisible, as are all of his troops. Some even question his existence. Rarely are "artillery sermons" delivered in pulpits around our land anymore. How seldom are Satan and his demons even mentioned by name. In the liberal churches you will hear all of that explained away: *"This isn't like that!"*

What are we to believe—that he's a little creature with a red epidermis and horns, carrying a pitchfork and sitting like an imp on our shoulders? No! Our foe is brilliant. "Genius" is a better word. He's been studying you for years. He knows you thoroughly and plans the attack that will strike at your most vulnerable weakness in hopes of bringing you down. He exists for your failure, fall, and demise.

In order to step intelligently and wisely into the battle, we need clear marching orders.

The words of Peter come to mind. In the fifth chapter of his first letter we find words that sound like

marching orders for Christian soldiers. But the initial command is surprising. It is not, "Attack!" It is, "Humble yourselves" (v. 6). We need to understand, this isn't human strategy based on human strength that requires human giftedness, which will lead to human accomplishments. This is altogether contrary to what any of us would imagine. The Lord's marching orders are, "Humble yourselves." It's a picture of falling on your face before God in submission and trust. Trace that word back as far as possible, and you will find people on their faces before God. The word picture includes God's almighty, outstretched hand reaching across this universe, including this tiny little planet and including His church, which He brought into existence by His power and for His purposes.

He says, "Humble yourselves under my hand," which means you and I don't get our way. It isn't about getting what we want. When you humble yourself under the Master's hand, you humble yourself to the Master. It's about our doing what He wishes. It's what He plans that

matters. You hardly need to be told that everything in our society works against that message. No matter. The command stands: "Humble yourself under His mighty hand, that He may exalt you at the proper time" (v. 6).

There are rewards in doing as He commands. God is no divine sadist, watching people squirm and struggle and bleed, hoping to club them into submission. Don't go there. Keep in mind that God, our loving, caring, faithful, holy, and just God, has shaped a plan that will lead to victory, hope, peace, and joy. All of it takes shape under His mighty hand, as we surrender our wills to His. It happens under *His* hand. Get that. And under *His* hand we give up what *we* want. We surrender our wishes and desires, as we accept His plan. In the process, He is glorified. And because of His grace, many rewards come our way. The blessings just keep coming like waves on the seashore. And they come at "the proper time," because His timing is always right.

You say, "That kind of full surrender to another's plan makes me nervous."

Well, that's why there's verse seven: "Casting all your anxiety upon Him . . ."

"You mean I may not be able to get what I want?"

No, you won't get what you want. You won't have your way. If that makes you anxious, there's a simple solution: Cast all your anxiety on Him. Yes, all of it. When you do, you'll have a lot less struggle releasing your will to Him. You'll march into battle with far greater confidence and calm.

What I'm suggesting here is a totally different lifestyle. This will touch every part of your world. In the final analysis, it will lead to a 100 percent investment in Him.

Perhaps I'm hearing you say, "Well, I don't want to invest, say, my whole life."

Then let me cut to the chase: You don't really want Christ. That's right. *You don't want Christ.* You want a God who won't make such wholesale demands. That way, you can hear what you want to hear and do what you please. You want a God who makes you laugh,

makes you feel good, and says yes to your every request. You want a comfortable desk job, not a tough challenge on the front lines.

You say, "Man, this is getting serious." You're right.

Peter tells us to be sober, be on the alert, watch out. Follow your marching orders. The first one is clear: Humble yourself. And if you do, when the time comes in the battle, He will lift you up to conquer the enemy.

When our enemies struck America, I was both saddened and gladdened to see our nation fall to her knees before God and humbly ask for His protection. I was gladdened to see the Statue of Liberty bow her head in reverence and recognition of God once again. But I was saddened that it took such an evil, dastardly event to bring us down to where we need to be all the time.

We have received and accepted our marching orders: "Humble yourselves." Now we must find the courage to move out.

TEN
COURAGE TRANSFUSION

Be on the alert, stand firm in the faith,

act like men, be strong.

— 1 CORINTHIANS 16:13

THE CHALLENGE WE FACE is painfully obvious. Our foundations are in place and trustworthy. The Lord our God, being our refuge and very present help, relieves us of fear and worry. He is in sovereign control. He hasn't lost His grip on our times. Under His mighty hand we humble ourselves. And, in spite of our adversary's subtle and deceitful strategy, we are certain of this: *In the end, God wins.* What we need until then is a courage transfusion.

Please turn in your Bible to a single verse in

Why, God?

1 Corinthians, chapter 16. I want to give you eight words that I hope you never forget. I offer these eight words in four two-word commands. The four commands are found in verse 13 of 1 Corinthians 16: "Be on the alert, stand firm in the faith, act like men, be strong." Each one of these two-word commands deserves a bold exclamation point.

Here's the first command: Be alert! When Paul first wrote this imperative, he put it this way: "Keep on watching!" Clearly, the command tells us that our great need is to be acutely aware. It includes spiritual alertness, an awareness of the unseen, an understanding of the insidious, a quick perception of that which could be a part of the satanic conspiracy.

I'm not a witch hunter. Don't put me in that category. But as we have already established, there *is* a conspiracy against the plan of God. It has been going on since before the fall of humanity in the Garden of Eden. Satan hates God's plan, so he works against it. And the first thing the enemy would love for you to believe is that there really is no such thing as a conspiracy. It's there, nevertheless. Be on the alert when you read the newspaper. Pay attention to what *is* said and what *isn't* said. Read today's news magazines and watch today's news telecasts with keen biblical discernment.

It's time for discernment to kick in. Moms and dads, be alert to your children. Watch what they do, and pay attention to what they are saying. Employees, be alert to your bosses and how they are directing your steps. Bosses, be alert to the companies you are putting together and to the people you have hired. Christians, be alert to what is going on around you in the church, at school, in civic matters, among politicians, with the military, and in the Oval Office.

Be alert to what is said. Be alert to your surroundings, be alert to people who live around you. Pay attention to your own motives. Listen to your own words. Be alert when you listen to the radio talk shows, paying attention to what is *said*, and even more important, to what is left *unsaid*. Be alert!

Be aware of the bait that's being dangled before you that causes you to yield a little more in an area of weakness. Be alert to the fact that there is an enemy against you. When your day starts, apply EWO—Eyes Wide Open. From the moment your feet hit the floor, keep your eyes wide open. That way, few things will come as a surprise; you'll seldom have to admit, "Why, I would never have imagined such a thing."

A recent movie was titled "Eyes Wide Shut." I didn't see the movie, but the title speaks eloquently about today's culture. Our visual senses are bombarded with shocking, horrifying scenes in America—drive-by shootings, tornado and earthquake disasters, schoolyard assaults, planes plunging into the World Trade Center twin towers, trapped victims jumping to their deaths, body parts falling to the sidewalk in front of us, starving children, and on it goes. And what do we prefer to do? We close our eyes, we squeeze them shut, so we don't have to witness such harsh realities. We opt out. We deny the truth. We run from reality. In doing so, we close our minds to the enemy's schemes and attacks. We go through life with eyes wide *shut*.

In contrast, God says, "Stay alert!" Stay alert to biblical principles. You will read of them every time you open the Word. You will hear them every Sunday if you attend a Bible-teaching church. These biblical principles will guide your steps. Pay close attention to them. Remember them. Memorize some of them. Be alert! That's God's first line of defense for us. Be keenly and discerningly aware.

I am continually amazed at the dullness of many Christians, who will put up with a lack of truth being taught Sunday after Sunday. It's like the old prophet, Hosea, who said, "My people are destroyed for lack of knowledge" (Hosea 4:6). Another prophet named Amos wrote of " . . . a famine on the land, not a famine for bread or a thirst for water, but rather for hearing the words of the LORD." He wrote of people staggering from sea to sea looking for the truth yet being unable to find it (Amos 8:11–12). He didn't describe simply his own

times; he described the United States of America. Be alert to what you're not receiving from those who should be declaring God's truths. Be alert to what you're being told. Be alert to the ministries and other organizations you support financially. Be alert!

Second: Stand alone! It is rendered here in 1 Corinthians 16:13, "stand firm in the faith." Eugene Peterson says it this way in *The Message:* "Hold tight to your convictions." You may have spent years listening to preaching. Some of you have taught in Bible Study Fellowship, in small group studies in your home, or at the place where you work. Many of you are engaged as fine Bible teachers. Stand firm in the truth you are teaching. When necessary, stand alone.

Don't let it bother you that you are different. That's what makes you unique. It gives extra value to your intelligence. That's what puts you in demand. I will tell you from experience, the mentors who have shaped my life have all been uniquely different. None of them fell into the basic category of "dull." None of them bored me with the Bible. Their lives were lived on the edge. Some, admittedly, were a little weird, a little strange. But I loved it that they didn't blend into the background, like the majority. They stayed unique. That's what got my attention. They all lived above the level of mediocrity. Each one was so "different." That's what attracted me to them.

I thought of this when I was reading *Sports Illustrated* not too many months ago. One of their best writers, Rick Reilly, always writes the last page in their magazine. So every time my copy comes, I turn to the back first and read "The Life of Reilly."

The particular article that caught my eye was especially good as he wrote about one of my all-time favorite coaches, John Wooden, the former UCLA basketball coach. It was so good that I called it to the attention of my older son, and I said, "Here's a column worth following." He also brought it to the attention of many of his friends. It's called, "A Paragon Rising above the Madness," and it refers to more than-90-year-old ex-coach John Wooden, whom Reilly calls "the best man I know." He wrote:

There's never been a finer man in American sports than John Wooden, or a finer coach. He won ten NCAA basketball championships at UCLA, the last in 1975. Nobody has ever come within six of him. He won 88 straight games between January 30, '71, and January 17, '74. Nobody has come within 42 since.

There has never been another coach like Wooden, quiet as an April snow and square as a game of checkers; loyal to one woman, one school, one way; walking around campus in his sensible shoes and Jimmy Stewart morals. He'd spent a half hour the first day of practice teaching his men how to put on their socks. "Wrinkles can lead to blisters," he would warn them. These huge players would sneak looks at one another and roll their eyes. Eventually, they'd do it right. "Good, good," he would say. "And now for the other foot."

Of the 180 players who played for him, Wooden

knows the whereabouts of 172. The things he passed on to them he passes on to their children, on their little lunch bags, who will then roll their eyes. Words like, "Discipline yourself, and others won't need to," Coach would say. "Never lie, never cheat, never steal," Coach would say. "Earn the right to be proud and confident," Coach would say.

You played for him, you played by his rules: Never score without acknowledging a teammate. One word of profanity (psst), you're done for the day. Treat your opponent with respect.

He believed in hopelessly out-of-date stuff that never did anything but win championships. No dribbling behind the back or through the legs. "There's no need," he'd say. No long hair, no facial hair. "They take too long to dry, and you could catch cold leaving the gym."

That one drove his players bonkers. One day, All-American center Bill Walton showed up with a full beard. "It's my right," he said, as he towered over the Coach. Wooden asked if he believed that strongly.

Walton said he did. "Well, that's good, Bill, that's good. I admire people who have strong beliefs and stick by them, I really do. And we're going to miss you." Walton shaved it right then and there. And now Walton calls once a week to tell the Coach he loves him.[1]

If nothing else, maybe these words will encourage you to be different, to stand alone. That's what makes you great. Don't care how others run their companies; run yours right. Don't care if most of the people walk away from danger; you walk toward it. You do what's right. Don't lie. Don't cheat. Don't steal. Don't hang around with people who do. It takes courage to swim upstream, against the current. Do it!

Third: Grow up! If the first two haven't been strong enough, I thought I'd get your attention with the third one. Here are two words you may not have heard lately: Grow up! Paul says it like this: "Act like men." I know you're an adult. But age proves nothing. It's maturity that matters. This command urges us to be adults in things that matter, like taking responsibility, thinking clearly, and acting courteously.

I love the motto of the Ritz-Carlton Hotels. Cynthia and I are good friends with Bill Johnson, who, for a long time, owned the Ritz Carlton organization. They came up with a wonderful motto. While sitting among us at one of our Insight For Living board meetings, I looked over in Bill's direction and asked, "Can you give me the mission statement of the Ritz-Carlton?"

His response was instantaneous: "I sure can." He pulled a small card out of his shirt pocket and read, "We are ladies and gentlemen serving ladies and gentlemen."

Was I impressed! So, when Cynthia and I were staying for a few days at the Ritz-Carlton Hotel on Maui the following summer, the lady who made up our bed came in every day. She was so kind and extremely efficient. Remembering Bill Johnson's comment, I decided to ask her a similar question.

I said, "By the way, Maria, do you know the Ritz-Carlton motto?" There was no hesitation as she stood a

little taller, smiled, and answered, "Oh, yes sir. We are ladies and gentlemen serving ladies and gentlemen."

It had permeated from the top all the way through to the people who make the beds. They take their mission seriously. They're adults when it comes to being responsible. There's something great about being an adult, a real lady, a real gentleman. It helps you stand tall.

Did you know that this is the only place in all the New Testament where these words appear? "Act like a man." One-time-only words are called a *hapax legomena*, which means, "spoken once." Now, it's used in other ways in the Old Testament Greek Bible, but this is the only place where "act like a man" appears in the New. So this is God's unique message to all of us, as if He's punching His finger against our sternum. Isn't it about time you take responsibility for your own actions? When you do what's wrong, say it was wrong. You're the one who caused the problem? Admit it. That's what adults do. You tell someone you'll do something, then do it! Let's act like ladies and gentlemen. Ladies keep their word. Gentlemen are faithful and true.

It's childish not to want to change. My mind drifts to the two little grandchildren who were living in our home for a few months before our son Chuck and his wife Jeni moved them to their new home. The little show stealer those days was Jessica. (We call her Jess). She's a little red-haired doll and is absolutely adorable. On occasion back then she walked around in a dirty diaper. As a result, this little cutie spread the aroma everywhere she went.

And her daddy would say to her, "Jess?"

She'd say, "Yes. . . .?"

He'd ask, "Are you dirty?"

Jess would shake her head, frown, and say, "No."

Then he would say, "Well, what do I smell?"

"I dunno," she'd say as she walked away with a shrug. She just preferred to stay dirty. She totally ignored the need to get cleaned up! She didn't want

him to stop and change her diaper. Why didn't she want a change? Because she's just a little child.

Do you need a change? Since you're an adult, grow up and change! Don't tell me why it's hard. No one wants to hear you whine about how hard it is to change. If you can't pull it off, call on your Lord for assistance. If change means moving toward the right, you have no other option. Move. Otherwise you stay dirty and you get irritable, and you start to complain. We don't need more complainers. We need willing grown-ups!

People who are grown up keep their vows. They don't run around on their mates. Don't sneak around having an affair and try to rationalize your sin by telling your friends how tough it is at home. Nobody has the interest or time to listen to that. Everybody has it tough at home. They have to live with *you*, don't they?

Get your "stuff" together. Act like a man. Be brave and courageous as a lady. You're the only one on the sales force who's telling the truth? Good for you! Keep it up. God honors integrity, which is another sign of

maturity. When other people are responsible for good things happening, always give *them* the credit. That's what mature adults do. Servant-hearted leadership is wonderful to behold.

One of the greatest men who ever led a seminary is John Walvoord, who served as president of Dallas Seminary for thirty-four years. At this writing he is ninety-one years young. We had a great ninetieth birthday party for him. It was terrific. We sang, "Happy Birthday to You" with pipe organ and trumpet and a great Presbyterian "Amen" at our commencement chapel. It was wonderful. He stood there with a big smile, staring at everyone. Looking at him, I realized what a model of maturity he has been for many, many years.

I was telling that story to someone and they said, "Did you know that George Mueller, at age seventy-two, left the orphanage to his son-in-law? Mr. Mueller then went on eleven tours of the world and seven tours of Europe. He witnessed to the czar of Russia, the emperors of China and Japan, and the queen of

Denmark. He then went to be with the Lord at age ninety-five while preparing to preach the Word that evening." I call that living like a man.

We need ladies and gentlemen serving ladies and gentlemen in Christ. I warmly invite you to join the ranks. The times in which we live are tough, so they require tough-minded ladies and gentlemen whose hearts are tender.

Stay alert! Stand alone! Grow up!

Now the last command won't surprise you at all; you're all ready for it: *Get tough!*

I didn't say "mean." I said "tough." Look at the way it reads: "Be strong."

Have you ever played for a coach who wasn't tough? If so, guess what you did all season—lose! Great coaches are tough-minded; they attract people who do their best for them. Winning requires being tough!

If you're a preacher and you speak week after week, preach what *needs* to be said, not what others *want* you to say. You preach it until the day you die. Stand firm,

even if they don't want to hear it and finally run you off. That's your calling. If you're a counselor, tell the truth to people you counsel, even when they don't want to hear it. Truth sets people free.

Suppose a friend says to you, "You know, I have to admit, things aren't great between Bob and me at home. Our marriage isn't going anywhere. And so, wouldn't you know it, I met this guy at the gym. Boy, he is terrific. He's more my type. Matter of fact, we're going out to dinner tomorrow night." She thinks she's solving her problem, but you know better. She needs tough love.

Put your arm around her and say, "That's the worst thing you could possibly do. What you're getting into will only multiply your difficulties at home."

If you're a counselor and you have a counselee who comes in whining over something that's really sinful, don't shrug it off and say, "Oh that's okay. I understand. Those things happen. I'll pray that things work out." No. It's time to speak up. Tell the person to stop and help him know how. Tough talk works!

Sinning brings bondage. Caring enough to confront and speak truth will set people free. We're all freer as a result of hearing truth from the Scriptures. You're not deeper into your problems, wondering how you'll ever get out of this mess you made. God's Word is a lamp. Finally, you can see some light.

We're living in a world of people so twisted they make you think perversion is right. And if you don't think perversion is right, you're wrong. That's madness! The Bible calls it confusion. Call it that. I don't care if you're the only one thinking like that. It's part of doing what's right. Getting tough begins with being tough on yourself.

I was digging around a dusty old bookstore several years ago, and I came across a little volume on the life of the great composer Ludwig van Beethoven. He was some kind of man. He composed some of his greatest musical works after he lost his hearing. He ultimately went stone deaf. As the thickness was drawing a veil over his auditory nerves, he had to rely more and more on the feelings in his fingers. At times he would even rest his forehead on the piano to hear the vibrations of what was being played. At one time, in a frustrated moment, he slammed both fists on the keyboard and shouted, "I will take life by the throat!"

What great advice for life. Take it by the throat. Stay alert! Stand alone! Grow up! Get tough!

That's what we have to do both as Christians and as Americans. Now is the time for a courage transfusion. We have to be alert against the enemy. We have to stand alone against evil, even if others choose not to. We have to grow up as a nation—stand tall and act like men and women. And we have to be tough—not mean, not responding with evil for evil—but tough. Meeting the challenge. Taking life by the throat. Standing up. Standing tall. Standing firm. Standing together.

---

[1] Reprinted courtesy of *Sports Illustrated*: "A Paragon Rising Above the Madness" by Rick Reilly. SI., March 20, 2000. Copyright © 2000, Time, Inc. All rights reserved.

ELEVEN
THE LAST COMMAND

Let all that you do be done in love.

— 1 CORINTHIANS 16:14

ONCE YOU'VE IDENTIFIED THE ENEMY, gotten your marching orders, and plucked up your courage, then what? Surprise attack? Storm into battle with guns blazing? Climb into your planes and tanks and blow the scum away? "Come on, we're ready! What's the final command?" There is a fifth command—in verse 14. You thought I missed that, didn't you?

Here's the fifth and final one: Always love! Whiplash! That's not what we expected. That's not what we wanted to do. You're kidding, right?

"No, child. Always love. That's the final word. That's what I want you to do. Always love." *Always love.*

And let me tell you who needs your love most of all—your lost friends. Our problem is, we can't get along with, much less love, Christians. Then we try to haul our crippled principles to the lost world to keep them from drinking or smoking or cussing or gambling or whatever may be the dirty dozen on your list. And it doesn't work. Why not? Hey, friends, it's because they're lost. *They're lost.* I'm surprised more of them don't use profanity. I'm surprised more of them don't have affairs. They're lost! They don't need our oh-so-pious principles shouted in their faces. They need our Savior's redeeming love to embrace and hold them. Let true love find its way through all of these commands, and it is remarkable what a difficult target the enemy will have when he tries to take us on.

We're together in this fight. But we are only as strong as *your* link in the chain. We're only as alert as

you are on *your* watch. We stand only as tall as *you* stand when you're all alone. We are only as mature and wise as *you* are as a grownup. We are only as tough as you are when *you* face the enemy.

And we're only as loving and gracious as *you* are when surrounded by those who are neither.

Let's talk about that love.

It's the kind of love that lets a man put his two-month-old child into someone else's arms so he can try to help make sure that the doomed aircraft he is riding on is not used as a flying bomb.

The kind of love that makes a firefighter run into a teetering skyscraper in the hope that he can rescue the people trapped inside, only to have that building collapse on him and more than a hundred of his brother firefighters.

The kind of love that allows another firefighter to shrug off his injuries, saying, "Whatya expect? I'm a

New Yorker!" And then burst into tears, thinking of his fallen buddy, who has ten children.

The kind of love that creates a convoy of physicians and nurses heading for New York City, riding in ambulances and their own vehicles, not knowing how much help they can be, but just wanting to help.

The kind of love that causes people the country over to stop and give blood, because that's the only way they can help.

The kind of love that permits a community like ours to put aside everything to come together and stand against those who would harm our own.

This country, and the free world beside us, stands shocked and dismayed. We are angry, and justifiably so. We have been attacked by people with no desire but to make us afraid, to make us hurt, perhaps even to make us hate the way they do. Maybe they do this because they know no other way; I personally do not care for their motives. I know that whatever their ultimate

goals, they have failed already. They attempted to sow fear, and instead reaped heroism.

We are dealing with people who will die in order to kill, so great is their hate. But they are dealing with a people who will give their lives to save the lives of people they don't even know, so great is our love. In the end, how can they possibly stand against that?[1]

In the final analysis, it is the love that enfuses us with the courage to face the enemy down. It is the love of God coursing through us as conduits to the terrorized world that dries our eyes, stiffens our backs, and sends us out as soldiers and comrades and family—standing shoulder to shoulder and arm in arm for right and justice and freedom. It is the love that lifts the flag of faith high and leads heroic hearts into the heat of battle. It's this kind of love that wins the war, not hate.

It's the love that keeps us faithful and strong, even while we wonder, "Why, God?"

It's the love—the undaunted, unending, glorious, unbeatable, victorious love—that overcomes the enemy.

It's the love.

Don't you see it? Can't you feel it?

It's the love.

Selah.

---

1 Anonymous. "Let's Talk about Love."

EPILOGUE

THE HORROR OF SEPTEMBER 11, 2001, will haunt our minds and hearts forever. As the death toll rises and reports of the destruction from the terrorist attacks on the U.S. are more specifically identified, we cannot and will not forget. These deplorable acts are indelibly imprinted on our lives. And we, as a nation and a family, don't *want* to forget. But now is a time to look also at the other side of the numbers coming out of New York, Washington, and Pennsylvania. This is the sad but somewhat uplifting side that the mainstream media may not have reported yet—the survival rates and some positive aspects of the attacks. We all need this now.

The Buildings

The World Trade Center

The twin towers of the World Trade Center were places of employment for some 50,000 people. With the missing list of just over 5,000 people at this writing, that means 90 percent of the people targeted survived the attack. A 90 percent on a test is an A.

The Pentagon

Some 23,000 people were the target of a third plane aimed at the Pentagon. The latest count shows that 123 lost their lives. That is an amazing 99.5 percent survival rate. In addition, the plane seems to have come in too low to affect a large portion of the building. On top of that, the section that was hit was the first of five sections to undergo renovations that would help protect the Pentagon from terrorist attacks. It had recently completed straightening and blastproofing, saving untold lives. This attack was certainly tragic, but a statistical failure. Furthermore, the side of the building hit was on the opposite side from where the highest-ranking leaders, both civilian and military, have their offices.

The Planes

American Airlines Flight 77

This Boeing 757 that was flown into the outside of the Pentagon could have carried up to 289 people, yet only 64 were aboard. Thankfully, 78 percent of the seats were empty on this horrific day.

American Airlines Flight 11

This Boeing 767 could have had up to 351 people aboard, but only carried 92. Thankfully 74 percent of the seats were unfilled.

Epilogue

United Airlines Flight 175

Another Boeing 767 that could have seated 351 people only had 65 people on board. Fortunately it was 81 percent empty.

United Airlines Flight 93

This Boeing 757 was one of the most uplifting stories yet. The smallest flight to be hijacked with only 45 people aboard out of a possible 289 had 84 percent of its capacity unused. Yet these 45 heroes stood up to the attackers and thwarted a fourth attempted destruction of a national landmark and our leaders, saving untold numbers of lives in the process. Their names will go down as freedom fighters in the annals of American history.

In Summary

Out of potentially 74,280 Americans directly targeted by the terrorists, 93 percent survived or avoided the

attacks. That's a higher survival rate than heart attacks, breast cancer, kidney transplants and liver transplants—all common, survivable illnesses.

We grieve the loss of those who perished, along with their courageous families, friends, and coworkers. And, in honor of their memories as great Americans, we refuse to live our lives in fear of these or any other terrorists. They will not win. They had a 93 percent failure rate! The odds are obviously against them, because we have the one and only true God on our side. May God continue to bless America—the land of the free and the brave.

BENEDICTION

May God be gracious to us and bless us
and make his face shine upon us. *Selah.*
—PSALM 67:1, NIV

A Prayer for Calm

LORD, *we are gathered around our Standard. We are bowed before our great God who offers His peace* when so many panic. You are our refuge, our chasah. Rivet that into our minds. Show us how to pause, and let it sink in. Remind us of your power and presence when the songs in the evening change into the fearful tears of the night. Remind us of that when the shrill ring of the phone awakens us. Remind us of that when we sit down and read the morning headlines. Remind us, oh great God, that You are our refuge and strength. Remind us, even when we don't understand the why of what's happening, that we have no reason to fear, that we need not be moved, and that our future is never uncertain with You. In the strong name of Christ, our Almighty Lord, Amen.